The Passive Income Blueprint Social Media Marketing Edition:

Create Passive Income with Ecommerce using Shopify, Amazon FBA, Affiliate Marketing, Retail Arbitrage, eBay and Social Media

By

Income Mastery

The information herein is offered for informational purposes solely, and is universal as so. The presentation of the information is without contract or any type of guarantee assurance.

The trademarks that are used are without any consent, and the publication of the trademark is without permission or backing by the trademark owner. All trademarks and brands within this book are for clarifying purposes only and are the owned by the owners themselves, not affiliated with this document.

Table of Contents

Before we begin I have a free gift for you from Russell Brunson - for those of you that don't know Russell Brunson is, he's the man that created Click Funnels. In my opinion it's the best funnel website out there and it has also helped create the most millionaires. Any form of passive income you are going to build, you will 100% need to leverage funnels of some sort. If you're reading this book, then you want to be the best in your industry. This book will give you the play by play to have people PAYING you for your advice. I am able to give you his best selling book for free right down here. I only have a few copies left so please get them while you can. Just click this http://bit.ly/giftfunnelbook

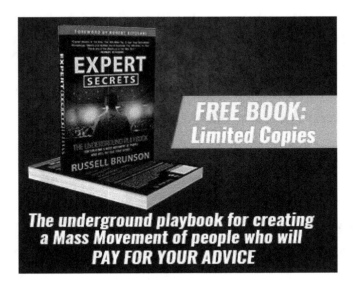

Introduction

As connectivity through the internet increases, so does our ability to talk to one another, share our ideas and make new friends all from the comfort of our own home. While the media often likes to discuss the pitfalls and dangers of social media, we must not forget that this unprecedented connectivity gives us a tremendous power. As business owners, artists and marketers, we now have the ability to bring our products, our ideas and our dreams to those who would respond positively. In 2019, there are more opportunities than ever before to market through the power of social media. All it takes is an understanding of the forces that drive social media and a genuine earnestness to connect to people who are looking for your services.

This book will take you through the many steps required to become a social media marketer, from sharing the basics of finding an online niche, to learning the ins and outs of using most popular social media platforms. You will learn how to effectively use Facebook, Instagram, YouTube and other social media outlets to boost your brand's performance as well as find people who are looking for products like yours. If you are a small business owner, an artist or an independent operator who is looking to increase sales, gain a following and connect to likeminded people, then read on!

Chapter 1: Top Reasons to Use Social Media When Building a Business Online

You may have some hesitations about using social media. Perhaps you have heard in the news all of this talk about how bad social media can be for people, or maybe you just aren't quick to adopt new technology. Whatever the reason for hesitation, it is understandable. But while there are so many stories out there that are so quick to herald the doom of humanity thanks to social media, there is one thing that we often take for granted: connection.

Before Facebook came along, people did not see or hear from one another unless they called or lived in the same area. With the advent of social media, long-lost friendships were suddenly rekindled. Family members who lost touch found a way to talk to each other quickly and effectively. Phone numbers change, people move across the country, but their names stay the same. Social media brought people together in a brand new way. Connections were made that will now last a lifetime.

There are challenges that we will face, due to the unintended consequences of such an increased level of connectivity, but the fact remains that people can now connect in ways unheard of centuries past. There is much to be excited about when it comes to social media, especially if you are a business owner. You can now sell your wares to just about anyone online, regardless of their location. You don't have to depend on expensive television or radio ads to get your product in front of people. Marketing has never been better, thanks to social media. Below are several more reasons to use social media for the purpose of marketing!

Reason 1: It Builds awareness

Simply put, having an active online presence through various social media outlets increases the chance of your message coming across a potential customer. The internet is a wide place and a great number of people use it daily, so the mere fact that you are actively using social media greatly increases the chance of people becoming aware of your business and your brand.

Reason 2: You control your image

Every business has a reputation, both offline and online. When an individual is looking for information about a company, they search online. If you don't have a social media presence established, you won't be able to take control of your own image nor the narrative surrounding your business. Instead, whatever people are writing about you through third party websites, such as Yelp or Google Reviews, will be the only thing out there. By having an established social media presence, you can actively work to create the image for your company that you want and ensure that people see what you want them to see, rather than whatever random images are out there.

Reason 3: It encourages engagement

Social media is purely designed for engagement between both the business and the consumer. Before the advent of things like Facebook or Twitter, engagement only happened when a customer was inside the store, talking with the owners or employees. Now, a customer or interested person can interact with the business any time they like. If they have questions or concerns, you're free to answer them as quickly as possible. You could run promotions or create marketing trends that get people to share your links with one another, increasing the size of your potential market.

Reason 4: You get to know your target audience

Understanding your customer is one of the most important parts of running a business. Whether it comes to innovation, successful marketing techniques or simply creating a good product, having a keen insight into the mind of your customer is key. Through social media, you can get to know your target audience simply by observing their posting habits and how they respond to your own posts. On top of that, you'll even be able to gauge upcoming interest in products by either polling them or just showing previews of what is to come. This will help you plan ahead in terms of marketing for the release of a brand new product.

Reason 5: You stay in your customer's mind

In today's connected economy, thousands of products, ideas and services pass in front of a user's eyes on a daily basis. It can be easy for a customer to forget about the services and goods that you offer, simply because of the deluge of other things vying for their attention. However, when you have a regular social media presence, constantly dripping posts and conversations about your products, your company and your vision for the future, you will be subtly keeping yourself on your customer's mind. How many times have you seen an ad for a product and thought to yourself, "oh yeah, I forgot about that?" There are many things competing for both attention and the customer's dollar. By using social media to continuously capture their attention, even if it is just for a short while, you will begin building credibility as a brand. And, when the customer is ready to purchase or use a service, that constant drip may be the thing that brings them to your business!

Reason 6: It's not a huge investment

Marketing can cost some serious money. Working with an independent ad agency is not cheap, nor is purchasing television or radio ad space. However, social media advertising has revolutionized the advertising world because it is significantly cheaper than traditional advertising efforts. On top of that, the time investment is relatively low, thanks to automation services, you can schedule posts and advertisements in batches, saving you valuable hours of work. The analytic systems that social media platforms utilize will also allow you to get the most out of your advertising buck, as you can constantly evaluate the performance of your ads. The investment is significantly smaller compared to other traditional methods of advertising.

Reason 7: It's easy to learn

One of the purposes of this book is to help you understand just how easy it is to learn social media marketing. While it may seem complicated, especially if you're not the type to use social media, it is important to remember that all of these systems are designed by companies looking to make for the easiest user experience. All it takes is discipline to stick with it until social media becomes second nature to you. It is not nearly as hard as it looks.

Chapter 2: Establishing Yourself as An Influencer

In social media terms, an influencer is an individual who has a strong enough following that they are able to influence how other people see products, ideas and services. They are considered to have strong marketing abilities simply because of how closely they work with their own fanbase. An influencer has a strong relationship with their follows, often engaging with them in a deeper way that speaks to them. This creates a powerful bond of trust. Then, all an influencer has to do is give their seal of approval to a product and their followers will quickly click the buy button.

Traditional celebrity endorsements aren't nearly as efficient as influencers, primarily because celebrities don't have two-sided relationships with their fans. The relationship is entirely one-sided. So while a celebrity might be able to pitch for a new grill on television, fans of that celebrity might feel some skepticism, because it is nothing more than a paid endorsement. It is different with an influencer, however, as the relationship goes both ways. The influencer communicates closely and personally to the fan and as such, earns that extra trust.

Becoming an influencer yourself is a great way to earn the trust of your fanbase and increase loyalty amongst them. In addition, it also makes you an authoritative voice in the field that you have chosen. This increases the chance of new customers looking at your business and products.

The Secrets of Becoming an Influencer

Secret 1: Caring and connection

The core secret to being an influencer is one principle: human connection. Above all else, an influencer is someone who has a strong relationship with their followers. Without that relationship, you won't have influence over anyone. So, really, the most important thing to remember is that you should cherish and care for your followers. When questions are asked, reply to them earnestly and honestly.

When comments are made, either negative or positive, respond appropriately. Be kind and caring towards those who take the time out of their day to communicate with you.

Secret 2: It's about them, not you

When marketing online, it is very easy to become self-centric. The idea that social media marketing can help generate revenue can sometimes be too exciting for a business owner and as such, they spend most, if not all, of their time, talking about their own products. However, this isn't a great way to make friends. Think about it, do you want to spend time talking with someone who only talks about themselves? Marketing narcissism must be avoided at all costs.

Instead of constantly plugging for your own stuff every single post, instead, focus on asking questions, driving engagement and learning about your followers. Have a conversation that goes back and forth. Don't waste their time and yours by constantly posting about your products over and over again. If anything, it just makes you look concerned only with your business and not with your followers.

Secret 3: Provide value

Influencing is really about providing value to customers and followers alike. Value is defined simply as anything that your target demographic will find useful to them in their daily life. It can be anything from entertainment, to education, to answering difficult questions that they have. Followers are always looking for the greatest amount of value online. Depending on your market, they might find different things more valuable than others. For example, a pest control business will provide a significant amount of value by creating posts about how to deal with certain types of pests. Their customers aren't looking for funny videos or cat pictures, rather they are looking for solutions to the pest problems that they are having.

By providing value to your followers, you will create more trust and generate goodwill on their end. This also increases both your authority and credibility, which expands your role as an influencer.

By focusing on creating valuable posts that either inform, education or entertain your followers, you will be signaling to them that you care about them.

Secret 4: Connect to other influencers

Chances are, you won't be alone in the market you're working in. If that's the case, then there will most likely be other influencers in that field. But don't look at these other influencers as competition, rather, look at them as potential allies. When it comes to online promotion, you can never have too many friends. As long as you have something to offer another influencer, such as credibility or information, you should reach out and try to establish a relationship with them. Something as simple as following them, commenting on their posts or in certain platforms, such as Twitter, retweeting them can work to create a relationship with them. Over time, you both may be able to mutually assist one another and expand both your audiences. This can be done in a number of ways, such as running an exclusive promotion for that influencer's followers, writing a guest post or asking them to write a guest post for you or even going on their podcast or YouTube show.

Of course, it is important to look at the other influencers in that field as people and not just a means to an end. Don't expect them to do things for you just because you asked. Instead, work to provide value for them as well and create a mutually beneficial relationship. Build a friendship and do what you can to assist them in their endeavors.

Secret 5: Be a person

While you certainly have a business to run, if you want to become an influencer, you should be willing to at least put a face to the brand. This will help people see you more as a person and less as just another soulless company out to squeeze as much money out of customers as possible. Be honest and personal, share your own feelings and opinions. Of course, there are some caveats to this. You don't want to overshare and you certainly don't want to breach any uncomfortable subjects with your opinions. Instead, try to find a balance between company and person. People should see that your business is an extension of your own creativity, your dreams and your passion.

Mistakes to Definitely Avoid

Mistake 1: Inappropriate Behavior

There is no faster way for an influencer to lose their status than for an inappropriate comment or remark online. The most important thing to remember is that once something is online, it is there forever. Some people may post something offensive for only a few seconds before reason takes hold and they quickly delete it. However, someone out there has most likely taken a screenshot of it. You don't want to be someone who loses just about all of their credibility and goodwill for a single comment. Therefore, it is of the utmost importance that you steer clear of any kind of negative behavior towards others online. No insults, nasty comments or anything that can be perceived that way. Always take a minute to reflect before sending anything inflammatory online and ask yourself if there is any reward to what you are choosing. There usually isn't.

Mistake 2: Failure to disclose

Relationships between audiences and influencers require a strong amount of trust on both sides. Some influencers may end up promoting products that they have been paid to, either through endorsements or just simply cutting a check. Failure to disclose any type of compensation for promotion is inherently dishonest. An audience deserves to know whether your actions are of your own volition or if you are being paid or compensated by someone else to do so. If you fail to disclose this information and your followers find out, that trust will be broke and you will be looked at as a shill. Of course, when running a business, you might not run into this problem too often, but sometimes business will look to swap reviews with each other, offering to give you 5 stars in exchange for you to do the same. Those types of arrangements are unethical and should be avoided, if you wish to have trust and connection with your audience.

Mistake 3: Dishonesty

Along with failure to disclose, there is nothing worse than an influencer who is being dishonest with their followers. As a business owner, there is an expectation that your claims are verifiable and backed by actual evidence. When a customer purchases a product from you and they discover that you have either exaggerated or outright lied about the product's abilities, you run the risk of losing all credibility. The most important thing that an online business can have is credibility. People are taking risks when they buy online, especially when it's from a business for the first time. Be as honest as possible when promoting or discussing the products. If there was a major shipping delay in an order, be forthright about it. Dialogue is always better than silence, even if you aren't sharing good news with your followers.

Mistake 4: Purchasing engagement

Some people who want to become influencers might decide that it would be beneficial if they boosted the number of followers that they have. By using a third party system, they might decide to purchase followers or for a set number of "likes" for a post. This might seem like a great way to make it appear as if you have a large following, but in reality, it isn't actually doing much for you. Followers who aren't real people won't be able to engage, share your content and aid in promoting your work. In other words, if you have 1000 fake followers, you aren't an influencer because those followers won't do anything. Avoid services and companies that offer to boost your social media presence or turn you into an influencer through these shady tactics. At the best, you'll swell up numbers but have nothing substantive and at the worst, you could get busted by the social media platforms who have explicit rules against such practices.

All in all, becoming an influencer requires a strategic plan, patience and a willingness to engage deeply with individuals over the process of several years. There is no quick path to suddenly becoming an influencer who everyone looks to for guidance. It happens with one follower at a time. So be patient, focus on creating value and above all, look for a genuine connection with the people who follow you. A single person converted into your tribe, who follows you and looks to your brand for guidance is more valuable than ten regular followers.

Chapter 3: Starting an Online Business Using Social Media

If you're starting from scratch, perhaps starting an online business for the first time, you may find that the sheer amount of options are overwhelming. The internet has plenty of tools to get started and thanks to the endless amounts of guides, tutorials and websites out there, you may end up feeling lost in the flood of information. This chapter is to help serve as a general guide to getting started in the online business world, with a focus on developing a social media presence in the long term.

Finding Your Niche (And Your Market)

An online business has one significant advantage over local brick and mortar stores: the niche. When it comes to starting a brick and mortar store, you'll need to consider things such as storefront location, what is popular in that city, what sells the most, etc. With rent being so expensive, if you pick the wrong product type, you won't even be able to cover the cost of the building.

However, for online marketing, things are much easier. Since there is no "local" population to worry about online, you can be sure that if you find the right niche, you will be able to direct customers from all over the world to your shop. The trick, however, is finding a niche that sells well, attracts customers and is unique enough to avoid direct competition with larger companies that can both undersell you and out promote you.

Finding a niche market is probably the most difficult part of running an online business. If the market is too small, you won't move enough products to be able to turn a profit. If the market is too large, you will undoubtedly have bigger competitors who will be cheaper and more efficient. Therefore, it is of the utmost importance to locate the proper niche through a series of simple steps that will help you build a thriving business.

Finding a Niche

Step 1: Identify Your Own Passion

Marketing and selling is difficult if you don't have an actual passion for the products you are selling. Running a business is a serious commitment and if you aren't passionate about what you are making, you might find yourself growing quite sick of it after a while. In addition, the task of marketing and sharing through social media will ring hollow, since you don't have an actual love of the products you are pitching.

Therefore, the most effective way to build an online business is to find something that you genuinely care about. Passion shows, especially when it comes to advertising. If you can't get excited about a product, how can the customer?

Step 2: Evaluate competition

One of the major drawbacks to online commerce is the fact that you're not alone. There could potentially be other competitors in your field and they may have significantly more resources or credibility than you. What you don't want is to move into a space that is overcrowded, or dominated by a major corporation that will hog most of the pie. Instead, you want to find areas where the competition is fairly low, but the demand for the niche product is relatively high. This isn't easy and will take a bit of research on your end.

Evaluating competition simply requires the use of search engines and keywords to find online stores for products. The first page of the search engine will always be your biggest competitor in the field. For example, if you are thinking about starting an inflatable pool business, you will want to search for terms that a customer would search, such as inflatable pools for sale, or cheap inflatable pools. These search terms are what we call keywords. Keywords are the primary way that a business is found through a search engine.

By using keywords in your search, you can find potential competitors and evaluate the strength and size of the market. With the help of analytic tools, such as Google Trends, you can even see how many people have been searching for that term over the course of the last few months. A keyword that has a high number of competitors indicates that you should establish a niche elsewhere. A keyword that yields medium to low competition and a high amount of people searching for the term can indicate that you can establish a market in that area.

Keyword research is a necessary part of not only identifying your competition but also your target market. If a lot of people are searching for what you have, but there is a low amount of websites providing that good or service, you have identified an underserved market. This is the perfect spot to set up your shop and begin working to meet the market's needs.

Step 3: Differentiate Your Product

One way to find your niche is to focus on the differentiation of your product from the others on the market. Figuring out how to do something cheaper, more efficiently or differently with the same product will help set you apart from the hundreds of other products like it. The more you can differentiate your product, the more niche it becomes. This will aid you greatly in branding your product. By creating something that is different and using advertising to help consumers know what makes your product different than competitors, it will set you apart from the others. Differentiation is a must, especially if you are entering a market that is full of tough competition.

Step 4: Narrow Your Market

A niche is all about targeting a narrow market, preferably one that is underserved in the online space. This means you'll need to narrow your demographics and focus on hitting only a specific group of people. While it would be wonderful to have a product that will appeal to everyone, the truth is that you will get more mileage out of specificity.

By creating a narrow, specified demographic that you plan on targeting, you will have a better chance of getting quality customers who will convert and purchase your products. Niche marketing is all about finding the few people who will buy, rather than putting your ad in front of a large group who will simply ignore it.

This might seem a little counterintuitive at first, but think about it. You have a limited advertising budget and a limited amount of time. By narrowing the market and targeting only a specific demographic, you will be getting the maximum return on your investment.

Narrowing requires research. Searching consumer reports, finding out which gender makes the most purchases in the field, determining the age and spending habits takes a bit of work, but that will help you hone in and create what's known as an avatar. An avatar is a personification of the ideal customer. This is the person you want to find online, the one that you want to see your ads and purchase your goods. For example, if you're running a small, specialty bait shop for fishing, your avatar might end up being a middle aged man with a stable career, who spends most of his time watching fishing shows and spending his disposable income on fishing gear.

Thanks to the hyper-targeting methods of various social media systems, you can reach and connect with these types of individuals, getting your message in front of them while saving both time and money. Putting a fishing ad in front of 10,000 people who don't fish isn't nearly as valuable as getting your ad in front of 100 people who do.

Have a few specific avatars in your head as you begin to work. When creating an ad campaign, ask yourself, which avatar are you trying to reach with it? Some products might appeal to different groups and demographics for different reasons, which in turn will influence your advertising campaigns. Rather than have one generic advertisement designed to reach three groups, you could develop three specific ads meant for each avatar.

Starting Up Social Media:

Once you've done the legwork, determined what products you are going to sell and who your demographics are, it's time to begin preparing for your social media platforms. You'll need to set up a profile across all of the platforms that you wish to use. We will cover how to market on each of the major social media platforms in later chapters, but there are simple, universal principles that cover creating a profile just about anywhere.

Profile Tip 1: Use consistent branding

You should have a high quality logo and banner that is used on each profile that you set up. A customer should be able to go from your Facebook to your Twitter page and be greeted with the same images on both. Visual branding is important to get customers to create a strong association between the colors that you use and the products that you sell. This means you must stay consistent across the board. If you use a banner on one profile, you should use it on all other profiles.

Profile Tip 2: Have a clear message

In about sections, you should have a clear and concise description of your company or your product. Focus primarily on the benefits they confer and try to keep the descriptions as short as possible. The message should be conveyed at a glance. Most people will quickly click a link or look at an "about page" for only a few seconds, so get the crucial information out as quickly as possible.

Profile Tip 3: Stay professional

Your profile should include all relevant professional details, such as where your store is located (or the website) what times you operate, etc. Avoid jokes, pointless details or vague instructions.

Profile Tip 4: Have keywords in your description

Keywords, as mentioned before, are one of the most important parts of online marketing. When people search online, they often type in specific strings of keywords in the hopes of finding what they are looking for. By including keywords organically into your descriptions, you can help aim search engines towards your company. But it is important to have a balance with keywords, as some people go overboard, wanting to jam as many as possible into a description, but most search engines are on the lookout for such tricks and tend to ignore them. So a description of your business might read "We here sell only the best fishing bait for grouper." This is great because it includes a keyword that includes specifics "fishing bait for grouper." If someone were to write "We here sell all the best fishing bait, bait for grouper, grouper bait and all other types of bait for grouper," not only does it look tacky, but it also doesn't fool any search engines. Try to incorporate specific keywords as naturally and as organically as possible.

Profile Tip 5: Make them all at once

As you will see in this book, there are plenty of social media options for you to choose from. When you have selected the platforms that you wish to operate on, it would be a best practice for you to create all your pages and profiles all in one go. That way you are able to keep things consistent, copy and pasting the descriptions to one page to another. You will remember where you put all of the logos and banners and won't struggle with procrastination when it comes to making more profiles later. Most importantly, you will be able to compare all profiles at the same time and ensure they are all uniform and consistent with your brand.

A Word About Keywords

Keywords are the backbone of all types of online marketing, paid, social media or otherwise. If you wish to be successful in your business endeavors, then you simply must learn how to master keywords in all aspects.

Search engines are how anything is found online. As we've mentioned above, when a person is looking for something, they will first type a set phrase into a search engine. The engine will then look for the most relevant information that it can find and then bring forth a compilation of results, ranking from most relevant and popular to least relevant and popular. The first page of Google, for example, is one of the most important places that a search result can show up on. People who are searching for a subject usually select the first few results on Google. Only those who can't find what they are looking for go past the first page.

If you wish to be found when people are searching, you must learn how to research the proper keywords. Keywords can be the life or death of your product, regardless of where you are promoting it.

Even paid advertising relies on the right keywords in order to target the appropriate audience. So if you wish to find success, you will have to learn how to research keywords effectively.

The first thing to consider with keywords is popularity. Whatever market you fill will most likely have generic, large keywords that are utilized by larger, stronger companies than you. Since search engines are looking for not only relevance but also popularity, this means those companies usually stay at the top of the front page. You don't want to try to compete for that space, it's simply too difficult for a small business to be able to do so. Instead you want to work to find niche phrases that people are searching for, ones that have considerable competition. But how exactly do we find these keywords? By using keyword search programs.

Keyword research should be a major part of your marketing strategy. You should be willing to devote quite a bit of time to find the right keywords that you will be using in your descriptions for products, in your ads and on your website. To aid you in this process, you will want to use professional tools that are designed to help you track keywords. These tools will show you how many people are searching for said keywords, help you plan out what keywords to use and most importantly, recommends keywords based on what information you already have.

These tools usually need to be purchased, but that is simply the price of doing business. If you have the right keywords for your products, you will be able to drive organic traffic through search engines to your products. This practice is known as Search Engine Optimization or SEO, for short. SEO often gets a strange reputation amongst those who are unfamiliar with the practice. Either SEO is pronounced to be dead due to changes in the way search engines work, or people assume that SEO requires some kind of unethical, black hat type of hacking.

In truth, SEO is simply optimizing your content, your product descriptions and your website so that people have an easier time finding it when searching online. By picking the right keywords, using good long and short-tail phrases that are relevant to the product description, you will be edging out the competition.

It is important to spend time reading up about SEO practices. There is a lot you can do to help improve the visibility of your content and as search engines are updated, the practices can change. It would be wise, however, to steer clear of services that offer "SEO optimization" and make all sorts of big promises. Most of the time, these services tend to use outdated or unethical actions that don't help with anything other than wasting your money.

While there are companies out there that can legitimately assist with optimizing websites and content for SEO, it's better that you at least learn the basics, so that you can identify if such services are necessary. A lot of the basics can be done yourself. Most importantly, with the nature of the ever-changing ranking systems used by search engines, you will need to stay up to date constantly, so you know if your current SEO is still effective.

In the end, keywords are the lifeblood of good advertising. If you aren't able to determine which keywords will attract your target demographic, you will be missing out on a lot of organic traffic and struggle when it comes to developing a targeted market for paid advertising. Find a good keyword tool, learn how to use it properly and then give as much time as you can to collecting the right keywords for your company and your content.

The Importance of Consistency and Tone

Keeping a consistent message across all platforms is important if you want to convey a specific type of image of your brand to people. Remember, in today's online economy, brand is extremely important. If you want to be able to sell your products, you will need to develop a strong brand. And the key to any good branding is consistency. This comes down to simple things, such as choice of colors between ads. Figuring out which colors represent your brand is important, and then when you have, use those as your primary colors in visual design. Once a typeface has been chosen for your brand, stick to using that typeface for any ads with lettering.

You want to stay consistent so that people begin to quickly identify your brand. Think about the iconic Coca-Cola colors and letters. The moment you see that combination, your brain understands almost instantly that you are looking at an ad for Coke. Changing colors constantly, using different typefaces and lacking consistency can confuse your customers. Sometimes, they may even mistake you for being a different brand. This will hinder all of your efforts to foster trust towards your brand, simply because the customer won't realize your ad as being associated with your company, which means all of your brand work was for nothing. Stay consistent with your images, keep the same colors and typeface, no matter what.

Tone is another important part of effective branding. Your product will fulfill some market need and as a result, the tone should match the demographic you are targeting. If you are selling something fun, then a light, casual tone is important. Making jokes, sharing memes and goofing around is an important part of that brand image. But if you are selling something that targets serious, professional individuals, then you would advertise in a professional manner.

What's most important with tone is that it is maintained across all of your platforms. Having your tone shift from platform to platform can be jarring and confusing for readers who follow you on multiple social media sites. For example, if you are goofy and irreverent on Facebook, but ultra-serious on Twitter, people will receive mixed messages about your company. Instead, try to stay consistent as possible, staying on point with your company message and avoiding compromising how you present yourself in any way.

Chapter 4: Monetizing Your Audience

In order to monetize an audience, you must first be able to show that your products or service provides value to their lives. The central conceit to all good marketing is that you must provide value and in turn, people will respond to that value by making purchases. Marketing is not a zero-sum game. When a person purchases a product, it is because they believe that the product will enhance their lives in some way. So really, monetization is a win-win scenario. The customer wins because they get something that will provide value to their lives and you win because you gain a sale.

However, most people are discerning with their money. In order to convince them to buy your products, you'll need to move them through a funnel, gaining first their attention and then their trust, which then leads to a potential sale.

The internet is a big place and there are thousands of things that vie for a potential customer's attention. But attention is almost akin to a currency in the world of online marketing. If you wish to monetize your audience, you will first need them paying attention to your products, ads and pitches. This can be done through one of two ways: content creation or targeted advertising.

Content Creation

Relevant content helps capture the attention of potential customers and gets your branding directly in front of them. People are always looking for value online and content that provides them with the greatest amount of value means that they will also be paying the most attention to that content. If you want to be an excellent marketer, it means you will need to be willing to create interesting, relevant and engaging that either educates, entertains or engages your audience.

This type of content can greatly vary, but for the most part, it is freely available for consumption online. If content is not free, then it is a product. The reasoning behind this is simple: if you create free and interesting content, you are not only capturing attention from your target audience, you are also building up trust and goodwill. If a person becomes a fan of the content you provide, they will have a much bigger chance of converting to a sale than if they were unfamiliar with your brand entirely.

Of course, content must be of good quality and relevant to the interests of your audience, if you are going to be able to build up trust. Creating content that is outside of your target demographics interests runs the risk of attracting audience members who won't be able to convert, effectively wasting your efforts.

So what are some types of content that can aid in educating and monetizing your audience? There are plenty to choose from:

Blogs

A blog is a great way to get a steady amount of web traffic to visit you. Creating a blog is fairly simple and you can have it as a part of your website, allowing for visitors to naturally click on it to learn more about the company and the people behind it. When thinking of creating blog content, simply try to focus on helping your customers as much as possible. Don't treat your blog as a platform to advertise, because that doesn't really help anyone. They're already on your website, so they know what your company is about. Instead, provide value to them by writing good content that engages or educates them. If you can keep a follower consistently visiting your blog, week to week, chances are they will end up converting at some point.

Podcast

A podcast is similar to a blog, although it requires a bit more of a time commitment and a bit of investment in terms of the mic and other equipment necessary to run a show. However, if you are able to create interesting and engaging podcasts that generate a following, you will have a much higher conversion rate than if writing a blog. Podcast advertisers such as MidRoll find that people who listen to ads on their podcasts can have a conversion rate as high as 61% which is just phenomenal.

Video Content

Video content is another great way to provide value to consumers. By creating videos that provide solutions to specific problems or contain entertaining skits that people enjoy, you will be able to build a following of your own brand. Of course, the drawback here is that out of all the forms of content creation, making video content is the most complicated. However, if you are handy with a camera and have some ideas of what people in your market are looking for in a video, you should give it a try. Creating a YouTube channel where people can find helpful videos can quickly turn into conversions, especially if you have good demonstrations of your products available for them to watch.

Visual Content

Art, illustrations, infographics and memes are all great types of content that might not directly convert people, but will provide you with a steady stream of images to share through social media. Taking time to actually develop these types of content provides you with visual material that you can use as much as you like. On top of that, when sharing them through social media, there is a chance that others reblog or repost what you've made, which expands your reach and has a chance of bringing more people to your social media page or website.

What if I can't produce any of this content?

If you find yourself lacking the skills, time or even the creativity to create the content above, you have two options. The first is that you focus entirely on targeted advertising. While you may be able to generate plenty of sales that way, you are missing out on the ability to passively bring in a following. The second option would be to hire a freelancer to help develop content for you. Thanks to the online gig economy, websites such as Upwork allow for business owners to hire freelancers to develop content for them for a fixed rate. Then, you can use that content as your own and use it to help generate more interest in your products.

Targeted Advertising

The second way to monetize your audience is to use targeted advertising. While social media itself makes for good, organic ways to build awareness of your product and have conversations with potential customers, there are some drawbacks. The biggest is that social media outlets often want businesses to purchase ad space, as that is how they make money. Facebook provides a tremendous free service to the world, but they generate revenue mainly through selling ad space to advertisers. This means that they don't want to see businesses using their services for free.

Algorithms are designed to prevent businesses from allowing unpaid posts to reach a wide audience. So while creating a steady stream of content is useful for passive conversion, the truth is, without paid, targeted advertising, you won't really have that strong of an impact on social media. The good news is that social media advertising is fairly cheap and you only pay when viewers click on the ad, something known as paid-per-click or PPC.

Targeted advertising is the best way to actively monetize your audience. By putting direct ads in front of them with strong calls to actions, imploring them to look at your goods and make purchases, you will be able to begin converting your followers. The best part about targeted advertising is that it unlocks analytics, which will allow you to see how each ad performs, even down to the age and gender of the people who clicked on your ads. We will cover how to run Facebook ads in the 6th chapter.

Earning Trust

Awareness is one part of the equation when it comes to monetization. The second part is trust. In order for you to be able to sell products or services online, you must also be able to gain the trust of the user. In general, trust comes from an established brand, a good track record and policies that are meant to help soothe the nervousness of a new purchaser.

The fact is, buying things from a new store online is a risk. A customer doesn't really know if what they are ordering will actually show up, what will happen to their personal information, etc. We've all heard horror stories of online transactions that have gone bad in one way or another. As a business owner, one of your biggest goals should be to gain the trust of potential customers.

This can be done in a number of ways. The easiest way to gain trust is customer reviews that are readily accessible to those doing research. A group of five-star ratings on a website, a quote from a reliable review website or even a video review from a popular influencer can go a long way. Be on the constant lookout for ways to incorporate positive reviews of your product into your marketing, as a way to reassure your customer.

Another way to earn trust is to have a simple, money-back guarantee. Most products or services offer these as a way of both enticing a customer to make the purchase, but also a way to show that the customer's satisfaction is of the utmost importance. Sure, some customers might be finicky enough to make a purchase and then demand their money back, but for the most part, it is meant to help consumers find you as a business that they can trust. And that trust is worth a few returns a month.

Create an Email List

One of the most important aspects not only of social media marketing, but in all types of marketing is what is known as lead generation. When you want to sell your product, you will need to have a lead, something that directs you towards the right customer to sell to. There are many different ways that you can generate leads, mostly through using paid advertising to find the proper demographic who would be interested in your products. But how do you retain leads? Through an email list.

The email list is one of the most basic and vital parts of monetizing an audience. While your audience will grow through the work that you do, creating and sharing content, you will want to find a way to contact them directly, for the purpose of advertising products. The fastest and most direct way to contact anyone online is through their email.

However, the email is also something most users hold closely. Unless signing up for a service, people generally do not share their email addresses with advertisers. This is logical, because as everyone knows, getting spam can be irritating. If you sign up for the wrong service, you may find yourself suffering from a deluge of special offers that clutter up your inbox and make it harder to find the things that actually do matter.

So how exactly do advertisers manage to get a hold of their audience's emails? Well, they can go about it by a number of ways. The first is to acquire the email as part of a conversion step. For example, if the customer has decided to purchase one of your products, you can give them the option to sign up for your newsletter, which then grants you permission to use their email for marketing purposes.

Another method of gaining emails is to offer some kind of deal in exchange for a newsletter sign up. The most common method is to create a free product that is sent to them after they sign up. Such products can be either physical or digital. Most companies find that offering a free ebook usually gets interested leads into signing up.

Once you have an email, you now have permission to send them special offers, updates and news about your company and your products. In other words, you have been given a brand new method of marketing. Best of all, since the person is clearly part of your target demographic, you don't have to worry about your email falling on deaf ears.

A collection of emails that you've gathered is referred to as an email list. Expanding your email list should be one of your major priorities when building your marketing engine, second only to gaining direct conversions. Building an email list isn't difficult either, below are the steps necessary to create one.

Step 1: Find an email list service

The task of collecting, tracking and sending emails can be a cumbersome thing if done all by yourself, but fortunately, there are professional services out there that allow for creating email lists. These services are usually free, up until you reach a certain number of emails, after which you will be asked to upgrade.

These services allow for ways to store collected emails as well as run campaigns, tracking not only the amount of emails that you send out, but how many people click on them, what time, who clicks on links within the emails, etc. There are plenty of services to choose from, but since you're just starting out, we would recommend using MailChimp, as they work well for beginners.

Step 2: Create a list

Inside of your email list service, you will be able to create a specific list. This will be where all of the signed up emails will go. You will want to make sure that you divide all of your lists up by category, especially if you are operating multiple business endeavors. Name the list after the brand that you will be representing with your emails.

Step 3: Create an incentive

People won't just give away their emails for nothing. Most everyone knows that when they give an email, they will be on the receiving end of marketing emails. However, the good news is that if they are interested in what your company has to offer, they might be willing to accept those emails and even read them. You will want to create an incentive that will be appealing enough to your target demographic to give you their email.

This often involves the creation of something special, be it an ebook, a special discount code or some other incentive that they will receive in exchange for signing up for your email list. This incentive doesn't have to be big or flashy, but it should be appealing enough to your target demographic that it would motivate them to make the exchange. Then, you will have their email to add to your list and they will get a neat present from you.

Be cautious when it comes to developing an incentive. Some marketers get a little too ambitious when preparing and can end up creating an incentive that is simply too attractive or too general. This can bring in low-quality leads, people who will sign up purely for the sake of getting the gift and then unsubscribing immediately. You also want to avoid creating an incentive that appeals to people outside of your target demographic. Remember, the purpose of creating an email list is for marketing purposes. If you have a bunch of emails that are outside of your target demographic, you most likely won't see any conversions from them.

Step 4: Create a landing page

The landing page is where you will offer the incentive in exchange for the email. Usually, the landing page is just a simple sign up form that extols the virtue of the free product and then has a call to action, urging the reader to sign up now.

Landing pages can be created either using landing page hosting companies, or simply making your own through your website. Whichever you choose is really up to you, but you will need to make sure that you have connected your email list service to the signup form, so that any email captured is put directly into your email list.

The landing page design should be simple and specifically designed to get the email address. Don't try to do anything else with the page. In fact, most landing pages don't even have a header or a navigation bar that leads away from the website. Instead, they simply focus on showing a good display of the free product, gives the reasons why a person would want it and then points them to sign up. Less is more with a landing page, the more details that are there, the more distracted a reader could become. Instead, keep it simple, short and to the point.

Step 5: Create an effective opt-in on your main site

After you've made the landing page, which is solely for the purpose of directing traffic, you will also need to create the ability to opt-in to your mailing list on the main site. This can be as simple as placing a little sign-up form on the bottom of your homepage, offering the product in exchange for an email or it can even be a pop-up banner.

As annoying as they might be, pop-up ads do have some effectiveness, provided that they aren't aggressive, hard to close or offensively colored. There are free services out there that help with creating pop-up ads for your mailing list, such as

Sumo. This helps to create effective pop-ups and track metrics, so that you are able to tell if people are clicking through an signing up.

Despite all conventional wisdom about the matter, the truth is, good pop-ups do work. As long as the ads you design aren't irritating, you have a decent chance of getting a click-through rate of around 2% of people visiting your page, which is pretty good for something that is absolutely free.

Step 6: Direct the audience to the landing page

Once you have created the incentive and the landing page, all that is left is to work on capturing emails. You may want to share your special offer with your current audience by posting the link on your social media outlets. This will hopefully generate traffic towards your page and get you sign ups. But once you have already informed your core audience about this new special offer, you will want to continue to expand that precious email list.

The best way to increase the size of your email list is through targeted advertising, using one the social media ad systems, such as Facebook. This

is paid advertising but will work wonders in generating leads that you can then directly market to, for free!

Once you've made your email list and it has been populated with enough people to start marketing, you might be tempted to just start sending out emails, but there are some do's and don'ts of direct email marketing that must be adhered to.

DO: Send special offers

People need to receive some kind of value from your newsletter, or else they will quickly unsubscribe. Sending valuable, email only special offers is a great way to not only drive sales up but also helps your customers see that your email is valuable. This will help encourage them to stay subscribed and will reduce the amount of people who unsubscribe after sending an email.

DON'T: Spam them

Once you have a customer's email address, you must treat it like a precious, fragile gift. If you

treat it too roughly, it will break and the customer's trust in you will be lost. Sending constant emails, three to four times a day won't promote your business as much as it will just annoy them. Even if these emails contain special offers, no person is going to want to receive that much email a day. Instead, try to treat the customer with respect and keep the amount of emails that you send to a minimum.

DO: Share news about your company

Emails don't always have to be for the purpose of selling. Some people sign up because they are genuinely interested in the growth of the company, their vision or passion. It is useful for branding purposes to share good and interesting news of your company with customers, so that they see what positive things you are doing.

DON'T: Purchase emails from other companies

Email marketing is permission oriented, but you may find that some companies may be willing to sell email lists to you. This shady practice can be problematic for many reasons, but the biggest is that

the invasion of privacy will quickly cause concern among those who receive your emails without consent. They will unsubscribe quickly and most likely feel agitation towards your brand. And besides, the leads provided by these people who offer to sell certain email lists tend to be extremely low quality.

DO: Use analytics to track email performance

When you send out emails, you should be able to see how many people are opening them, how many links are clicked and by how many people. These numbers allow for you to track performances of emails and make adjustments to the emails that you are making. Sometimes bad email design, invalid links or uninteresting offers can sabotage your efforts to gain conversions. By tracking, you will be able to keep a close eye on which emails are performing the best and which are performing the worst.

DON'T: Hold onto emails forever

Ideally, you want to have a higher engagement rate from the users who have subscribed to your email list. Over the years, as you send out campaigns and emails, you may end up realizing that there is a bottom pool of users who simply don't engage. They don't open emails, they don't click on links, yet they haven't unsubscribed for some reason. You should cull these subscribers from your list every now and then, just to make sure that your analytics don't end up skewed by a large base that probably doesn't even check their email anymore.

Chapter 5: Utilizing Facebook for Marketing

Out of all the different social media platforms, Facebook is the biggest, most used and the strongest when it comes to targeted advertising. You may find that you would prefer to use other types of platforms, such as Twitter or Pinterest, which is fine, but you should still at the very least have a developed Facebook page for your business.

Facebook has over 2 billion users actively using the platform a month. Furthermore, the majority of those users primarily use Facebook through mobile apps, such as phones or tablets. With such a strong online community, it would be a bad idea to simply ignore Facebook.

Creating a Facebook Page

Making a Facebook Page is different than creating a user profile. The page will be the profile of your business. People who like a Facebook Page become followers, which means that when you post, your post will appear in their feed. Although, as discussed before, algorithms prevent your post from reaching everyone who has liked your page, especially if you try posting multiple times in a day.

The Facebook Page is necessary if you want to run Facebook ads, as that will be linked to your advertiser account. The Page also allows for you to do a host of different and useful things to help connect to and engage more with your followers and customers.

Creating a page is simple, all you need to do is select the drop down menu from Facebook and select make a page. From there, you will be given all the instructions necessary to create a page for your business. After you've filled in all the information, set up your profile and put in the proper links, you can move on to the next important part of your page: getting likes.

Getting More Facebook Likes

When it comes to running a business, Facebook likes are actually quite important. A page like does several things for your business, such as:

- Shares the individual's activity in their feed, potentially sharing your page with other people
- Allows for you to target them directly with promoted posts and Facebook ads
- Aids in creating a look-alike audiences for a wider reach with Facebook advertising.

So if Likes can be valuable, what is the best way to go about getting them? The first step would be simply to inform current customers, friends and those who would be interested in your new page. You can invite people to like your page specifically, which can help boost your general numbers at the beginning. However, you should be careful with this. It may be easy to go overboard and get a large number of friends to like your page, but first ask yourself, will this person actually convert? Will they be willing to purchase my products? You want the majority of your Likes to be from quality followers, meaning people who will respond and interact with you.

This means you might not want to invite the whole of your Facebook friends to Like your page. Getting a few hundred just to start isn't a bad idea, but don't take it any further. After your first initial push, only focus on inviting relevant people to like your page.

Another great way to get Likes is to be constantly putting up content that will be shared by others. This can be either your own content, or memes created by others and are in circulation. Be careful when sharing content, that you don't claim any of the content as your own, but feel free to contribute in circulations of jokes, memes and other entertaining visuals.

It is important to stay consistent in your posting, but don't go overboard. In general, you'll want to post only 1 post a day. Creating multiple posts in the same won't help increase exposure, thanks to Facebook's algorithms. Instead, try to make one quality post a day, five or six days a week. This will ensure the highest level of reach which can generate new likes.

And don't forget, the goal of Facebook isn't purely to generate likes. Many marketers sometimes get too fixated on the idea that they should focus their energy and time on getting as many likes as possible. While likes have their use, they are not the end step. The end step is to get a sale. A like is nothing more than a tool to get that sale. They should come over time, organically and through simply promotions on your end. Don't give into the hype by focusing on getting as many likes as possible. They will come over time as your product grows in both size and popularity.

Creating a Facebook Group

A Facebook Group is similar to a business page, with the exception that it functions more akin to a chat board. Everyone within the group is free to post content, questions or ideas. Furthermore, groups can be set to private, public or even secret, meaning people don't even know of its existence until invited.

This can allow for you, as a business owner, to give your customers a direct line to discuss your product with not only yourself, but with other users of the product. Groups are a great way to get the engagement of those who are interested in or passionate about your products.

Setting up a Facebook Group is easier than making a page for your business. You simply click on the dropdown menu and select, Create a Group. From there, you will have the option to name the group, invite people and set the privacy settings. Then afterward, you can go to the Edit Group settings to fill in the important details, such as the group's description, type, etc.

A Facebook Group is good for answering questions and concerns of customers. But it should not be treated as a way to market to people directly. Most folks have no interest in being directly marketed to, especially if they join a group to discuss ideas and converse with like-minded people. Instead, look at a Facebook group as an opportunity to foster dialogue, have good conversations and care about the needs of others. It will help build a community around your product and show to the people that you view them as more than just bags of money.

Messenger

Facebook Messenger is the instant messaging service that allows for people to directly contact you. This live chat feature can be great for answering questions quickly or addressing concerns about a product's features. Facebook requires that Messenger is installed as a separate app on your phone, if you wish to be able to chat on your mobile, so it is recommended that you download the app if you want to be able to answer questions quickly.

However, some questions can be answered automatically. You might not have the time to answer every single person's questions, especially if the information is readily available for them to consume. If that is the case, then you might want to consider using a Chatbot.

A Chatbot is a specially developed AI system that can be installed into your business page's messenger app. Then, after specific questions are asked or if orders need to be made, the chatbot will be able to respond effectively, saving you time as well as increasing the times that your business is available to chat to customers. You could be sound asleep at 3 in the morning, but a night owl sends a message wondering if you ship internationally. The Chatbot, if it has the right parameters, can quickly respond with the right answer. The customer is satisfied because they were answered quickly and you are satisfied because you can keep on sleeping through the night.

Making a chatbot isn't hard, but it does require a time commitment. You'll need to find an established chatbot system to use, unless you have a knack for programming on your own. Services such as Chatfuel, ManyChat or Flow XO are available, usually offering free services for beginners. If you find that you want a chatbot to increase response time, then these services will help and often require absolutely zero programming skills to integrate into your messenger.

Chapter 6: Using Facebook Ads

Facebook ads can be exceptionally powerful when used properly. Thanks to Facebook's data gathering ability, you can target people who would be interested in your product and as a result, increase your chances of getting a sale than through any other means of advertising. But this doesn't mean that you can just slap a few parameters into a Facebook ad and run it to make a fortune. Properly using Facebook Ads requires forethought, planning and above all, the ability to study analytics and adjust properly.

Getting Set Up

Setting up for Facebook ads requires you to create a business manager account. The Business Manager will be the homepage where you will be able to connect ads to your Facebook pages, run ads and most importantly, review the analytics that are provided after a successful ad run. In order to set this up, you just need to visit business.facebook.com and go about creating the Manager account. Once the account has been made and you have linked your account to your store page, you will be ready to begin creating your first ad.

Creating a Campaign Objective

When selecting the Create New Campaign option, you will be presented with a series of different objectives. These objectives are the end goal of your ad campaign. Facebook will track and perform differently depending on which objective you select. The objectives are separated into three categories: awareness, consideration, and conversion.

Awareness Objectives

Awareness has two options, brand awareness and reach. Brand awareness focuses on finding people who would have the biggest chance of being interested in your ad. This means it would display the ad in front of people who are not only interested in the brand but also have the highest chance of remembering your other ads. Facebook would then seek to display your ad in front of people who have the biggest chance of remembering your ad within two days. Those who have the greatest chance of remembering your ad will have a better chance of converting later on.

In other words, brand awareness campaigns help get your product and brand into a person's mind. Later on, when serious targeted advertising with a call for action appears in front of them, thanks to the groundwork laid out by your awareness campaign, they will have an easier time converting.

The other option is just reach. Reach is a simple matter of getting your ad in front of the highest number of people out there. This can be great if you just want as many people as people to be shown your brand at a single time. Like brand awareness, you'll want to use reach if you just want to people to simply become aware that your brand exists.

Consideration Objectives

Consideration categories are goals that require some kind of action from a customer, however, the action does not end in a conversion.

Instead, these considerations are meant to further educate or establish a relationship with a customer, moving them closer to the decision to purchase. The available considerations are:

Traffic

The traffic objective is what to select when you simply want to drive people to a specific page, most likely your website. If you want to increase viewers of your blog or website, without requiring specific types of conversion actions, traffic is the right selection.

Engagement

In Facebook terms, engagement means acquiring likes, getting people to share your posts or even having them claim a special offer. If you want to gain more comments and shares of a specific Facebook post, you would use the Boost Post option. A boosted post will show up in all of your page follower's feeds, which naturally increases people sharing posts or commenting on them.

App Installs

This is a straightforward option, clicking on the ad will take the viewer directly to the app store on their mobile phone. This is just a simple and easy way to promote an app if you are selling or giving one away.

Video Views

Video views functions similarly to engagement, with the exception that the point is to get people to watch your video content.

Lead Generation:

Lead generation is a necessary part of any type of marketing strategy. Sometimes you will have people who convert immediately, which is great, but other times, you may have people who express interest but for some reason don't pull the trigger on the sale right there. Lead generation allows for you to gain the personal information of a prospective buyer, so that you can email them later on. This objective allows for you to create a contact form so that prospective leads can fill out. Normally, you would offer some kind of deal in exchange for this type of information, such as a free ebook or perhaps a discount. All a person would need to do would be to click on the "sign up" button provided by the Facebook ad in order to gain the benefit. This will generate leads that you can follow up on later, directly marketing to them or even retargeting them with more ads later on.

Messages

The messages objective encourages users to connect to your business through the Messenger app and ask questions directly. This can be useful if you have a product that might provoke a few immediate questions, or if you are running an event and want people to be aware that they can contact you about any concerns or queries.

Conversion Objectives

Conversion objectives are essentially the end goal of any marketing plan, getting the prospect to convert to a customer by purchasing the service or product. There are three different conversion objectives available to use throughout your ad campaign.

Conversion

Direct conversion is tracked through something known as a Facebook Pixel. If you want to have an ad that takes a customer to your online shop, where they then make a purchase, you will need to install the pixel on your website so that you can track this behavior. A Pixel is essentially a tracker, an online cookie that follows the customer as they move from the ad to the website. Their actions can be tracked by this pixel, which then reports to Facebook and forms an analytics page, so you can see how many people specifically purchased items after clicking on the ad.

Creating a pixel is easy, you just need to go to the Events Manager section of your Facebook Business Manager homepage and select the Create a Pixel option. Once the pixel has been created, you'll need to inject it into your website, which is a little more complicated, depending on what web hosting site you are using. If you are using Wordpress, Shopify or other site builders like Squarespace, there will be different methods of placing the code on the website. Check with your site administrator or do some research to find out how to place the code onto your own website.

Once the pixel is in place, you'll have the option to track specific events, such as page clicks or when a purchase is made. This is how Facebook Conversion ads will measure effectiveness.

Without the pixel, you won't be able to directly correlate the clicks on your ad with the sales made. For example, if you had 100 people click on your ads, and 10 people bought something, the conversion rate would be 10%. However, without the ability to track the actions of your customers, you would have no way of knowing if those sales actually came from your ad. It could have simply been a coincidence.

This is why Facebook pixels are necessary if you want to run ads that direct people to make purchases on your website.

Catalog Sales

You can also sell your products directly through Facebook, by creating a catalog. There, you will be able to showcase and directly market your products without having to direct customers to your website first. If you have a storefront website, such as Shopify, you can even connect it to the catalog, making for a seamless transition from Facebook to the checkout. This objective simply puts the catalog right in front of the audience so that they are able to look at the wares that you have to sell and even browse through to see if there is anything that interests them.

As you can see, there are quite a few options when it comes to selecting a Facebook objective. Don't be overwhelmed, however! Learning to navigate Facebook ads is more of a skill than anything and every skill takes time before you are able to master it. Start out slowly, take it one step at a time until you are able to run basic ads without a problem. After that, you can begin to experiment and see the more advanced options that are available with Facebook ads.

What Makes a Great Ad?

Creating a great Facebook ad isn't hard to do. For starters, you'll need a visual element that is both striking, interesting and clearly displays what you are advertising for. If you aren't a graphic designer, don't worry, you have plenty of options. If you're a do-it-yourself type of person, try using Canva, a website that aids in the creation of good looking ads without the need for a graphic design degree. Otherwise, you can always just hire a freelancer on a website such as Fiverr, who will be able to quickly put together a good looking ad for you, using the specifications that you give them. It would be good to have at least three or four different types of ads made, so you can test them later.

Good visual design is key, but that's not the only thing that makes for a good ad. You will also need, clear and concise text that will capture the reader's attention. You only have a few seconds before a person loses interest, especially when they are scrolling, so make sure that what you write is an attention grabber. A clever slogan, a curious question or simply a combination of words that appeals to your target demographic can go a long way. Having bland, boring product descriptions or worse, some kind of corporate jargon that means nothing will quickly ensure that the reader keeps on moving. Good visual design gets them to look at your ad, but a quick, effective pitch will help them click on the actual ad.

Once you have good visual design and good copy, all that's left is a clear call to action. The ad must, in some way, call for the reader to do something. Whether it's to sign up, visit the website, buy now or read this, you must have a clear call to action that motivates the reader to actually click. Think of a quick, punchy way to call them to action. For example, if you are selling orthopedic running shoes you could make your call to action written as "Start running painlessly today!" or "Set your feet free now!" These are short and effective because they convey the core of your message and urges them to take action.

These three elements combined will allow for you to create a good series of ads for you to run. However, you won't know how effective each ad is until you begin to experiment with releasing them and seeing how they perform. At the end of the day, it doesn't matter how well crafted your ad may look, if it doesn't perform well when running, it's not a good ad. This is why you should try to utilize A/B testing as much as possible when you start out.

A/B testing, an option provided by Facebook Ads is where you run two different ads at the same time and then comparing them after they finish their run, to determine which one performs better. A/B testing, also known as Split Testing, is vital if you want to have the best possible ads. When starting out, you should be willing to use the A/B option, running ad A and ad B simultaneously, to see which design works better. This gives you flexibility and most importantly, real-time feedback from relevant audience members who don't even realize they are participating in a survey of sorts. Whichever ad performs better should be your main ad for the time being.

Running Ads on Multiple Platforms

Facebook's ad system allows for you to target multiple platforms. In general, you will always want ads running on both desktop and mobile. You will also have the option to select running an ad on Instagram, as Facebook owns that social media website as well. But the question is, should you? There is no hard and fast answer to this question. In general, Instagram users tend to be younger, so if your product doesn't target a younger demographic, it might be a waste of time. However, there is simply no way of knowing the effectiveness of your ad campaign without testing it first, so you may want to just do a trial run to see how Instagram ads work compared to running them only on Facebook. The analytics will be able to inform you of which one performed better and you may end up surprised with what you see.

Creating an Audience

Before you can run a Facebook ad, you will need to have an audience to target. An audience, in Facebook advertising terms, is a collection of facts, interests and demographics that make up your ideal customer. In other words, you will be taking the avatar that you've made and then turning them into a specific group of people to target with Facebook ads.

Making an audience is an easy process, as your first audience will be created through the Ad making process. You will be given a list of details to include for targeting, basic things at first, such as gender, age, location, language and then targeted interests.

When adding interests, try to be as specific as possible. The more specific you are, the better idea you will be giving Facebook's algorithms of the ideal person to put the ad in front of. Make sure to use the proper keywords that you've researched.

In addition to adding interests, you can also add connection types. For example, if you want to run a promotional that only people who have liked your Facebook page will see, you can select that perimeter.

This will, of course, shrink your audience size down quite a bit, and sometimes if the audience size is too small, Facebook will not be able to run ads for you.

Try to balance things so that you can get a well-defined audience, one that isn't too broad or too narrow. The closer you can get the little needle that measures the audience size to the green, the better.

Once you have tinkered around with creating your first audience, you will want to make sure that you save the audience, using the Save This Audience section. This will speed up the ad creation process in the future, allowing for you to quickly put in your prefabricated audience from the start.

There are many more options when it comes to creating an audience, however. One of the most important would be creating a lookalike audience. Once you've run a successful ad directing people to your website, your Facebook pixel will be able to inform Facebook of their interests, website viewing habits and consumer activities. You can then use this information to create what is known as a lookalike audience. Facebook goes out and creates a database of Facebook accounts that are similar to the people who visited your website, essentially creating a profile of entirely new customers who would be open to your advertisement.

Lookalike audiences are very powerful when used in conjunction with a Facebook pixel. The ability to gather data and then replicate that data gives you a serious edge when it comes to finding new customers to convert. When combined with simple campaigns meant to drive up traffic to your website, you can potentially identify more people to target at a later date.

Facebook Analytics

Analytics are extremely important when it comes to paid advertising. The ability to see who is engaging with your content, who is clicking through and how long they stayed will help you shape your future campaigns and expand into new markets. Most importantly, it helps you refine your audience targeting, which translates into more sales. The last thing you want is people who won't convert clicking on your ads, because each click costs you money.

With analytics, you can work to improve your numbers by evaluating the data provided. Let's take a look at what we can find out when we use Facebook analytics.

Accessing Analytics

In order to find out the analytics of your Facebook ads, you'll need to go to the Ads Reporting section of Facebook Business Manager. This will take you to the various ad campaigns that you have run and inform you of how the campaign performed. You will see several different statistics, which are what form the core of understanding how your ad performed.

Results

This section will show the end results of your objective, if you were attempting to get something like link clicks or downloads. This ultimately is the most important number, you want this to be as high as possible.

Reach

Reach is defined as the number of people who saw the ad at least one time.

Impressions

Impressions are how many times the ad was displayed total. Impressions are not necessarily unique, they could run in front of the same person multiple times.

Cost per Result

Here is where you will find out what you've actually paid per click or per impression. Since Facebook uses a bidding system, in order to price your ads, you may find that the cost of clicks varies. Targeting an extremely competitive field can result in more expensive clicks, while targeting a smaller, less saturated field may result in cheaper results. Overall, this is a number that you will want to keep as low as possible.

These are just the basic reporting sections that you see when you look at the performance of the ads.

You will see all of the ads run in a specific time frame listed this way, together, so that you can quickly compare and contrast, seeing which ones work better or were cheaper. However, thanks to the extremely advanced methods that Facebook uses, you can look at more specific demographic results to understand exactly what type of person engaged with your ad. Digging in deeper, you will be able to see which genders clicked the most, what age demographics interacted with your ad and even their location.

This can help you develop better, more focused ads. You may find that specific ads are more popular with a certain age or gender groups than others, which then allows for you to split your ads into two, creating a new one aimed solely at fixing the gender gap. Or you can simply remove one gender or age from your advertising bracket, knowing that they aren't as interested in your product.

The analytics of Facebook are deep and complicated. It would be good to spend time sifting through the data, learning as much as you can about exactly what gets recorded and how you can use that for your own benefit when it comes to selling more ads efficiently.

Retargeting

Once you have finished an ad run, you will have all the data you need to make a retargeting campaign. The internet is a very busy place and there are plenty of distractions available online. A person could click on your ad, take a look at your product and say "that looks great!" only to receive a text or email, leading them to forget entirely about your product. Retargeting helps you catch these customers who are close to converting but for some reason or another simply didn't.

And there are plenty of reasons why a willing customer wouldn't convert. Lack of funds, time constraints, forgetfulness or simply saying "I'll buy it later," can prevent you from not only getting a sale but from getting a loyal customer. However, thanks to Facebook pixels, you can see the number of people who visited your site and did not convert. This enables you to create a custom audience, targeting the people who visited the pixel but for some reason or another left without buying anything. Retargeting is helpful in reminding people who already expressed interest that your product still exists.

Since the pump has already been primed, awareness has been made, retargeting grants you higher conversion rates, provided the ads you are running are effective. Some companies even made special offers when retargeting those who clicked through, offering free shipping or a discount in exchange for a sale. Those small little details can sometimes be strong enough to motivate a customer to finally click the "buy" button and give you a sale!

In the end, Facebook Ads are one of the most powerful types of marketing tools that you can use online. The system is large and can be a little overwhelming at first, but just take your time. Run a few practice ads and don't worry too much about seeing a return right away. The better you become at using the system, the more results you will see. Some business owners become discouraged because they simply ran one or two ads, didn't see results and then wonder if it's worth it. But advertising is all about refinement and testing again. Sometimes you won't get good results, but that's okay! Because you are still collecting data in the process. In order to get those sales, you will need to have as much data as possible, you need to know what works and what doesn't. So make sure you stick with it for the long haul!

Chapter 7: Using Instagram for Marketing

While other social media platforms focus primarily on a mix between visual and written content, Instagram solely focuses on visual content. From pictures, to short videos, Instagram is the king of visual content. 60 million photos are posted each day on Instagram, and users love to scroll down endlessly, looking for interesting photos to like and make comments on.

Influencers are also the most prevalent on Instagram. While Facebook is more for personal collection and Twitter is for creating a dialogue between groups of people, Instagram is more focused on the content creator. Many Instagram models spend their days taking pictures, living glamorous lives and talking to their followers, creating a strong brand that enables them to live off their work.

If used properly, Instagram can have an excellent effect on your business. Sharing inside looks, previews of products and demonstrations are incredibly simple ways to promote your company. However, in order for these to be effective, you will, of course, need to begin to develop a following. Here are some ways to grow a following on Instagram.

Create a Business Profile

Before you do anything, you'll need to set up your current profile to be a business profile. This is simple to do, you just need to create a regular profile, then in the settings area, find the switch to business profile option. This will connect your Instagram profile to your Facebook account and from there you can run ads and access data from the account.

Add the link

You get one link in Instagram, the one that is present in your profile. That link needs to lead to the most relevant part of your business, such as your store website. This is crucial, because when people follow you, they will have an opportunity to click on that link organically, leading to your website. So pick the best possible link that you can.

Use Hashtags

Hashtags are exceptionally useful for getting people to land on your posts. Don't make the mistake of trying to create new hashtags, that is a privilege that people with an established following have. Instead, look at the popular hashtags that are trending and then tag your content appropriately. People often search by hashtags and posts are categorized by these tags. Try to follow what is trending, in order to attract organic traffic. Once you have identified what is trending, create posts that follow after that trend and use the appropriate hashtags. Instagram Insights, a business profile feature, will help you track the effectiveness of the hashtags that you have been running, showing how much traffic is coming to your profile based on hashtags alone.

Make sure, however, that you are fully aware of what a hashtag means before you try to utilize it. There have been unfortunate cases of a company attempting to co-opt a hashtag without realizing what it meant, only for it to be a terrible disaster. One such misstep was when DiGiorno, a frozen pizza company, decided to use #whyIstayed on twitter and gave the reason why they stayed. "You had pizza," they wrote, not realizing that #whyIstayed was about domestic violence and involved people sharing the reasons why they remained in dangerous, abusive relationships. This was universally criticized and the pizza company was forced to apologize for their insensitivity about the subject. Let that be a lesson to you, always make sure you understand the purpose behind a hashtag before you use it. Don't just look at the top ten trending hashtags and then slap it on your post.

Create Content

Reposting or using other people's content, as long as it is attributed to them, is a perfectly normal strategy on Instagram, but that's not a great way to build an interested following. Creating good, original content that is meant to be shared can work wonders for developing a good group of followers. The content doesn't necessarily have to be related directly to your business either. It can be motivational, beautiful, funny or just insightful.

You can follow current trends as well, looking at hashtags and then working to create content that is based on those tags. You can also follow seasonal trends as well, when the major holidays begin to show up. There is nothing wrong with following after a popular movement, as long as what you are creating is useful, entertaining or educational. This will help generate quality followers organically.

Follow relevant people

On some social media platforms, such as Twitter and Instagram, following someone back is considered to be a courtesy. So when you're first starting out, you should begin to find people who would be members of your target demographic and follow them. With any luck, they should also follow you back, which increases your follower size as well as gives you an opportunity to interact with them. Be careful of doing this too much, however, as there is a cap to how many people you can follow in a given day. That number is around 100 to 200 a day, 20 an hour. So follow only a few people every few hours, so that you don't risk having your account banned from following others. These measures were created as a way to prevent spammers and shady business practices from generating masses of followers.

Another thing to note is that you should also not bother following famous individuals or influencers *if* you are hoping that they will follow you back. These individuals tend to have a significantly smaller group of people that they follow. This isn't to say you shouldn't follow them, if you want to observe what content they are releasing and how they operate, that is fine. But the follow-back courtesy generally doesn't take place when you aim for the more popular users.

Comment and engage

Commenting and engaging in conversation with other users is a great way to create visibility for your platform. Your comments should be genuine, positive and friendly, as to encourage more dialogue with people. Try to make as many friends as you can through commenting on other's posts and contributing to a conversation. This can increase the chances of people following you out an appreciation for your thoughts and insights.

Share Behind the Scenes

Instagram and Instagram stories allow for you to share what is going on behind the scenes of your business. Showing your creative process, videos of products being designed or just sharing concept sketches can go a long way to engage people who are already interested in your product. Instagram Stories are pictures or videos that only stay up for 24 hours before being deleted. These are great ways to connect with your current fanbase, showing them short glimpses into the life of your company. This creates a stronger sense of engagement on your follower's end, because what they are seeing is exclusive. It will be around for 24 hours and that is it. This can be a very special thing, so make sure that as your following is growing, you are taking advantage of Instagram Stories to share what is happening behind the scenes.

Run Ads

Since Facebook owns Instagram, running ads on Instagram is a snap. You can easily create ads for Instagram through Facebook and run them exclusively on that platform. The principles for making an Instagram ad are nearly identical to the principles for making a Facebook ad with one core exception: visuals. Since Instagram is primarily focused on a visual medium, you will want to create custom visuals that will get a person to stop scrolling endlessly and look at your post. This means you'll graphic design that will catch attention above all else. You may have to spend a bit of time on crafting good visual ads, but they will be worth it.

Instagram is a fast, visual platform. You will need to stay committed to producing daily content and using the right hashtags if you want to grow. Authenticity is key on Instagram as well. Trying to be fake, overpromoting your products and talking to people for the sole purpose of selling to them later will quickly be noticed and as such, you will be discounted. Instead, stay genuine, kind and above all, focused on providing as much value as possible. Growing an Instagram following organically takes time, but it is worth it!

Chapter 8: Using Twitter for Marketing

Twitter is a platform for sharing content, having discussions and echoing other's sentiments, often by retweeting them on your own page. As a marketing tool, Twitter shines in its ability to reach many people at one.

The core nature of Twitter marketing is based around retweeting good content. Content that catches the attention of a follower will be retweeted, which means that the follower's followers will be able to see it. Some of those followers might retweet and soon, you could have a single post spread out across hundreds of different accounts.

Marketing through Twitter is similar to Instagram in a sense. While the medium is both visual and text, the principles are just about the same.

You want to amass followers by producing good content, and in turn, build trust and a relationship with those followers. Below are a series of tips on how to get the best out of using Twitter for social media marketing.

Post Often

Unlike Facebook, Twitter is a very busy platform. While Facebook algorithms allow for posting once a day in order to get visibility, the ideal number of tweets to make per day on Twitter is around 5 to 6. After that, visibility does begin to diminish. Usually, you will want to post during peak Twitter use times, which is around afternoons, or between 5-6 pm. You can use analytic software from a third party, like Buffer, to determine what the peak times are for your audience. By posting during these times, you maximize the chance of users seeing your tweets.

Retweet Others

Retweeting others is a great way to foster goodwill with the person that you are retweeting. It creates a good connection between the two users and in the process, encourages them to be reciprocal with your own content. You aren't always required to retweet other people's tweets and overdoing it can come off as spammy, so exercise discernment. Look for good quality posts of your followers to retweet.

You can also retweet with your own comments. This is a great way to begin a dialogue about the content that you have retweeted. Don't promote yourself here, of course, but instead ask questions, follow-up and work to foster more of a connection with the user. When people feel engaged with, they will begin to engage as well.

Respond to mentions

Since Twitter is based around conversation, your business may be mentioned occasionally. Setting up a keyword search that alerts you when your business is mentioned, or just paying attention to when someone formally mentions you by using your Twitter handle puts you in a good position to respond to their concerns quickly. This can be great for handling customer service problems that have occurred. Many times, if a user isn't able to get resolution through conventional channels, such as email, they take to social media. The last thing any company wants is to have someone badmouthing their business on Twitter, especially if their problem is legitimate. By keeping an eye out for these complaints, you will be able to quickly put out any fires and in the process, protect your brand from potential damage.

Create short-form content

Twitter excels at short-form content. With a character limit of 280, you have room to share a few ideas in a single statement. People like tweets because short, punchy statements are easy to digest and can spark a lot of thought. If you want to do well at Twitter, you'll have to learn how to craft good tweets. Usually, you want your tweet to reflect your company values and your passions. Keeping a consistent tone is important, but try to avoid being too formal and corporate. People are looking for close connection and corporate jargon that is cold and meaningless can often drive a wall between you and your followers.

Instead, stay warm, personable and humble. Use humor as often as you can when writing tweets. Stay away from offensive or tasteless jokes, but feel free to make fun of the things that are unique to your target demographic. The more relatable your words are, the more a follower has a chance of seeing your company as more than just another suit trying to sell them junk they don't need.

Exercise Caution

Twitter is can be a powerful social media platform, if used right. On it's best days, Twitter is a great forum where everyone can share their opinions with one another, engage in discourse and share the things in their life that they find interesting. On its worst days, Twitter can quickly devolve into an echo chamber that turns into an angry mob, turning its collective anger or wrath against something they deem as immoral or wrong.

It is important to tread carefully when using Twitter, as there are many things that can cause trouble for your account. The biggest one is any form of political stance. Due to the anonymous nature of the internet, there aren't direct consequences to being part of a mob that threatens or slanders the name of a business. While it might seem like a good idea to take a political stand on one issue or another, the divisive nature of Twitter will ensure that at least one side will come at you if they notice what you are saying. As a business owner, you should work to keep your account neutral, focusing on people instead of politics. This will save you a tremendous headache.

In addition, you should exercise caution when it comes to communicating with others. Avoid any kind of negative or aggressive stance with users. It doesn't take much for a person to try and start a spite fight, especially online. Resist the urge to get pulled into pointless arguments, disagreements or discussions that go nowhere. Remember, anything you post on the internet is forever. Don't let a heated exchange with some troll on Twitter harm you and your company.

Schedule Posts Ahead of Time

As a business owner, you probably have quite a bit of work to get done in the day. You might not have the time to sit down and write five quality tweets each day, let alone for every day in a single month. Fortunately, there are third-party management systems, like Buffer or HootSuite, that let you write tweets out in advance to be released at a specific time of day during the week. Instead of trying to work each day at a time, it will be far more beneficial if you take one day to prepare all the tweets for the week. Then, all you have to worry about is responding to people's comments and questions.

Advertising

Running ads on Twitter will be different than Facebook, primarily because the platforms are owned by different companies. So, if you decide that Twitter is going to be the major platform that you want to use, you will have to spend time learning how their advertising system works. Fortunately, while the platform is different, the core concept is the same. You will create an advertising campaign, using specific objectives and you are only charged when those objectives are met. The campaigns can range from gaining more followers, to promoting a specific app, to driving traffic to a website.

The key difference between Twitter and Facebook advertising is price. Twitter advertising is a bit more expensive, but at the same time, does have a higher click-through-rate than Facebook, meaning that more people actually click on the links provided. Of course, your mileage will vary depending on the types of ads you are running, what your objectives and what your budget is.

Overall, Twitter is a fine platform to run paid ads on, as long as you are focusing on Twitter as your primary platform. If you are juggling between Facebook and Twitter, you might want to consider using Facebook for advertising, as they are a significantly larger platform than Twitter.

Chapter 9: Using YouTube for Marketing

YouTube is one of the most popular video content platforms on the planet. Every day, five billion videos are watched as hundreds of millions browse through and watch their favorite shows. YouTube is a dominator of the online video market, anyone can upload a video and if they get enough views, they can even monetize their work!

As a social media marketer, you have two different opportunities to use YouTube. The first would be to create your own content and host it on your own channel. This can be a difficult and time consuming feat, but it will increase your audience size and give you a direct, free method of marketing products to people.

The second opportunity is to take advantage of YouTube's video ad system and pay to market through YouTube. This will give you a wide audience and since most ads are unskippable, will guarantee that you will have exposure. Let's explore how to make the most out of both opportunities.

Become a Content Creator

Content creators are big business on YouTube. Those who are able to gain a large enough following can even work on YouTube full time, taking in large checks from ad-sponsors who pay out the big bucks.

However, to get to that point requires a significant amount of time, a serious game plan, and more importantly, a willingness to work long hours and for years to accrue that big of a following. Most likely, as a business owner, your focus will be elsewhere. But that doesn't mean you can't build a following yourself!

By creating a channel that focuses on providing solutions to customers, showing off product demonstrations and helping with frequently asked questions, you can reassure potential customers of your legitimacy as well as the value of your product.

Putting Together Your Channel

When creating a channel, you'll want to think about the type of content that you will be producing. Try to sit down and create an outline of the different types of videos that you want to make. Some categories include:

- Instructional
- How-To
- Unboxing
- Product display
- Behind the Scenes
- Interviews
- Comedic sketches
- Troubleshooting Guides

From these categories, think about what you want people to visit your channel for. Do you want to draw in audience members with humor, in the hopes that they'll look at your more product oriented videos later? Do you want to create a video addressing a frequently asked question about how to put the product together? Any strategy is fine, as long as you are willing to develop a video schedule around that strategy.

Once you've figured out which categories of video you want to offer, you'll need to then go about actually creating the videos.

While video creation is outside of the scope of this book, we do have some general tips to offer to help increase your chances of getting a viewer to keep watching past the first few seconds.

Tip 1: Get to the Point

Solve the problem first, pitch to them later. Most people who are looking for solutions tend to be frustrated already, so don't compound the frustration by having 4-5 minutes of talking before you get to the actual solution to the problem. Instead, start your video off by just jumping straight into the point that you want to make. Don't focus on buildup, especially if you are making an FAQ or troubleshooting video. People come to YouTube looking for quick and efficient answers. By skipping all the "hi guys" or "today we're going to talk about…" you will actually be fostering more goodwill from viewers and will increase the chance of gaining subscribers on your channel.

Tip 2: Use performers if necessary

If you aren't good in front of the camera, if you struggle to get outlines or find yourself immensely uncomfortable being the spokesperson, then it would be a better choice to either hire an actor or simply use someone else within your company to be the performer for the video. With YouTube being a visual medium, there is an expectation for some semblance of decent performance ability in the spokesperson. A polished, articulate speaker can go a long way in keeping the attention of a viewer. And a lot of YouTube videos are personality driven. A little personality can go a long way, especially if the subject matter of your videos are n't especially glamorous.

Tip 3: Write a script in advance

For the first few videos, you might find it better to write out a script in advance, that way the performer has a reference point to run through. After a while, the spokesperson will probably gain the ability to speak extemporaneously, but if they are just starting out then having a fully developed script will be handy. In addition to improving a performance, a script also ensures that all relevant details are provided during the video. You don't want to accidentally skip important details and then only realize it during editing, well after all of the equipment has been put away. A script allows you to keep everything nice and tidy.

Tip 4: Don't worry about perfection

Developing videos for a YouTube audience takes time to master. If you worry too much about perfection, you will most likely struggle to produce anything in the beginning. Unless you are working with a serious video budget and have hired a production team, chances are your first few attempts will be less than great. But like anything, you will find the more that you produce, the better you will get. Create videos, put them out there and then take feedback as you get it. Remember, perfect is the enemy of good. Better that you actually release a flawed video than to waste hundreds of hours on a single video in order to make it "perfect." Because even then, once the perfect video is released, someone, somewhere will find something to complain about.

Tip 5: Take the comments with a grain of salt

You should be willing to listen to comments, after all, comments are how people communicate praise, dislike, frustration and feedback. However, thanks to the power of online anonymity, you can deal with commenters who are simply looking to cause trouble by trolling or insulting you. Indeed, YouTube comments have become the butt of many a joke due to the toxic behavior displayed by commentators. Therefore, you should be willing to look at all comments with a grain of salt, knowing that those who display especially hurtful or cruel remarks are just people looking to mess with you and cause you pain for no reason other than they find it fun. These are not valid forms of criticism and should be ignored.

Hopefully, you won't have to deal with these trolls during your pursuit, but if you do, remember one core principle: don't feed the trolls. Interacting with them, replying to their comments, fighting with them won't change their minds, it will only encourage them to mess with you even more. Worse yet, you may find yourself losing your temper and writing something you really shouldn't write online. As the old saying goes, "never argue with an idiot, they will only drag you down to their level and beat you with their experience."

Creating Ad Videos

YouTube advertising can be quite promising. With the ability to control your budget, paying only when your videos are watched and the large audience that uses YouTube every day, it is possible for you to get better exposure than some primetime television ads. The caveat here is that you are going to have to put some work into the video that you are making, it will need to look more professional than if you were simply making regular videos to post on your

YouTube channel. This means you'll need to have a budget, a decent quality camera and a good script that can quickly and effectively convey your intent to viewers.

Making a good ad video isn't a small endeavor and you will most likely want to hire professionals to write and produce the video. It doesn't have to be crazy expensive, but you can expect that video advertising will cost significantly more than advertising with still images. Then again, video advertising also has a much stronger reach, since, on YouTube, the audience is captive. If you are running 6 or 15-second ads that are unskippable, the viewer will be required to watch the ad, especially if they are on mobile. This type of exposure can be well worth the higher price point.

Getting set up with a YouTube advertising account requires you to have a Google Ads account. Since YouTube is a Google owned company, that means you'll be primarily working on the Google Ads platform to manage, review and launch ad campaigns.

In order to run a YouTube video ad, you will need to have the video itself already uploaded to your video channel. After the video has been uploaded, you can then select it, the target demographic and the budget for the ad run. After that, it's simply a matter of running the ad and watching how it performs.

YouTube Analytics

As you create content and run video ads, you will hopefully begin to experience an increase of subscribers. From your video dashboard, you will be able to access the analytics page, so you can examine as a whole the number of viewers you receive, the reach of your views and things such as top videos in the last month. Pay close attention the age and genders of your subscribers, this will help you get a general idea of exactly who is taking an interest in your videos.

You will find that over time, the more data that you have to work with, the easier it will be to think of what kind of content to create. For example, if you have been making a bunch of comedy videos, and a single how-to video, and the how-to is your top video across the board, while your comedy videos go unwatched, you should switch to focusing on how-to categories. Follow where the data is leading you. If certain types of videos aren't doing well, just drop them. You don't need to worry about producing underperforming videos, instead focus on producing more of the popular stuff. Give the people what they want, simple enough.

Overall, whether you want to create content so that you can drive awareness of your brand up and promote your products, or if you just want to make ads, YouTube is a great platform for any marketer who has the time and the budget for these larger productions. While the cost might be higher, the returns can be quite significant over the long term.

But just because people are following you on Snapchat doesn't mean you'll automatically have their attention. Chances are, if they are a daily Snapchat user, they have plenty of people they are following and that means you'll need to work in order to keep their attention. This translates to creating interesting video content, taking good photos and working to ensure that you are engaging with your followers.

Snapchat is a lot more of an active medium. With the nature of Snaps only lasting so long, you won't be spending a significant amount of time planning ahead for your content. You can only share videos and pictures taken with the Snapchat app, meaning that you will have to incorporate creating content throughout the day. Since snaps are short-lived, you will have to learn how to capture spur of the moment events, take quick photos that you think would interest your followers and plan ahead for what you want to snap. This is certainly a skill that takes time to develop, but over time, you may find that you enjoy the ability to share moments with your followers.

There are paid advertising options through Snapchat. However, when compared to the sheer marketing effectiveness of other platforms, such as Facebook and Twitter, Snapchat's paid ad system comes up short. In addition, the price points of Snapchat are significantly higher than Facebook or Twitter. There are some budget options for using Snapchat's Discover tier, but for the most part, Snapchat advertising is expensive and the ROI isn't terribly apparent, especially with the way the company is continuously changing. However, if you have a larger advertising budget and are looking to reach the young market, then Snapchat advertising might be worth the gamble.

Gaining Followers

Since you aren't able to gain followers through discovery on Snapchat, you'll have to develop other methods of generating followers. The easiest way would be to simply share with everyone on your other social media platforms that you are now on Snapchat. Show them your Snap handle or even upload a picture of your QR code, so they can just scan it right there.

If you have built a quality relationship with another social media influencer who has a strong Snap following, you might want to ask if they would be willing to promote you on their own Snapchat. This promotion is as close to in-app discovery as possible, because if they mention your handle to their audience, the people will be able to directly follow you without having to change apps.

Your website should also have your Snap handle listed along with the other social media icons, that way people who are browsing your site can find it quickly. If you really want people to know about your Snap handle, then you might want to even consider doing a Facebook awareness campaign, with your handle in the ad so that readers have access to it. However, if you do that, you'll want to develop the ad so that it gives some reason behind why people should be interested in following your handle. Perhaps by offering a special discount that is only available on Snapchat, such as a coupon code that can only be seen for 24 hours before fading away.

Uploading Good Content

Once you have a following, you'll need different types of content to keep them engaged with you. At the very minimum, you should make a habit of snapping once or twice a day, in order to make sure that you stay on your audience's radar. These snaps don't need to be polished, in fact, many people enjoy the raw nature of Snapchat. Instead, try to simply take pictures or videos of what you think customers would enjoy seeing. If you have a beautiful view on the way to work, Snap it. If someone made a terrible mess in the kitchen, Snap that too. Try to begin thinking like a photographer. Look for opportunities to capture in the moment stories that would appeal to your core audience.

In addition to slice of life pictures, there are other ways you can get your audience within Snapchat excited. One great example would be a contest or giveaway. Have users send you snaps of something relevant to your field and then after a short period of time, award the winner with some kind of prize. This type of contest can be excited and will drive up engagement with your followers.

Limited time offers, coupons and exclusive deals can all work wonders to not only drive sales, but also can expand your following, as word of mouth will pass along that only a specific deal can be gained through using Snapchat. Be sparing with these coupons, of course, you don't want to overwhelm your audience with only deal related Snaps, as that will begin to look too corporate and may cause a drop off of followers.

At the end of the day, Snapchat is a fantastic tool for getting to know your core audience better. The back and forth nature of sending pictures to one another and creating stories foster a sense of connection and unity that most other social media platforms are missing. But there is a higher time commitment with Snapchat than the others. You can't preplan content and you must actively engage with your followers throughout the day in order to maintain the relationship. If you are someone who prefers to be hands-on with your social media marketing, then this is perfect for you. However, if you find yourself wanting to plan content out, automate your services and respond to messages on your own time, you may find Snapchat to be too aggressive a platform to use.

Chapter 11: Using Pinterest for Marketing

While other social media platforms often cover a wide variety of topics and subjects, Pinterest excels as primarily a vehicle for sharing pictures of DIY projects, food and drink and arts and crafts. People are able to "pin" posts to their boards, creating collections that they then share with others. This allows for posts, also known as pins, to be rapidly shared between interested demographics.

Pinterest's primary user base is women, making up over 80% of the user base. With Pinterest being a highly visual medium, it can be quite reminiscent of a home and garden magazines. People who are browsing Pinterest aren't looking to converse with like-minded people, rather they are actively looking for projects, recipes, ideas. In other words, they are searching for something to spend their time or their money on. This makes Pinterest a great social media outlet if you are someone who is looking to promote your custom crafts or products that can be used in crafting, cooking or other types of home based projects.

So who should be using Pinterest for marketing? Primarily businesses that work with products that are visually appealing. Pinterest users often browse and pin with the thought process of "I'll add this to my wishlist." So, ideally, your product should be something that a user would find worth pinning to their board. Once pinned to a board, it stays there, constantly reminding the potential customer that the product can be purchased at any time. Furthermore, those who visit that user's board will also come across the pin. If they like, they will add it to their board, hopefully sparking others to do the same.

The potential for a pin on Pinterest circulating is quite high. The average amount of times a pin is repinned is 10, which increases the amount of organic sales that you can generate using Pinterest. The only downside to Pinterest is that it is a highly visual medium, which means you will need to develop visual content as the primary method of generating interest in your brand.

Using Pinterest

Using Pinterest is fairly simple to do. You will need to create an account, build a profile and then under the settings section, convert it into a business account. A business account will give you access to analytics as well as advertising tools that you will be able to use to increase the amount of people that you reach each month.

Once you have set up your business account and filled out your profile, you can then get ready to start creating pins! The first thing that you'll want to do is make a board. Your board will be the area where you store pins. Users can also follow your boards, so if they aren't interested in your whole business account, but they do like a single board, you still technically have a follower.

Boards are designed to cover certain topics, so make sure that when you make the board, you give it a good description that covers what you will be posting. People subscribe to boards specifically for the topics they cover, so don't try to create a catch-all board. Instead, you can create multiple boards for different categories, if they aren't related. For example, if you want to have product pins and then an inspirational meme pin, it might be better to separate the two into their own boards, unless they are directly linked together somehow.

Once you've made your board (or boards) you are ready to begin creating Pins! Creating a pin is easy enough. All you need to do is select the create pin option, add the image and then write a description. Keywords are extremely important here, as people find pins usually by typing in specific phrases and words into the search engine. The more specific to the target demographic the keyword is, the better. But as with all things, avoid keyword stuffing and try to instead incorporate keywords organically. Then all you need to do is add your Pin to the relevant board and you're good to go!

Some Tips to Remember

While you might be excited about the prospects of having a higher rate of customer acquisition through Pinterest, it is important to remember that this is still a social media site. This means you must be willing to interact with others, comment on posts, save other people's pins to your boards and be a general encouragement to others. Pinterest does allow for paid advertising, known as Promoted Pins, which can get your product pins in front of other people, so those should be the primary avenue through which you advertise. For the rest, it's the same as any other social media platform. Build relationships, establish a following and create value for other people.

You'll want to make sure that each Pin that you create has your logo present somewhere. This is to prevent people from taking your image, circulating it around the web and you not receiving proper credit. This watermark shouldn't be overpowering, just somewhere that makes sense on the image. This will ensure that even if someone does take your image and then share it with others on different social media sites, your brand will still be promoted.

Pinterest has a lot of mainstream business users. If you wish to increase your following and promote brand awareness, there is value in watching businesses that are similar to you. Spend some time looking at their Pinterest boards and observe what they do. Look at their promotion ratios, what type of boards they have, etc. And then, once you have a good handle on how they are promoting their own products, you can begin to imitate them. Of course, you will want to put your own twist on things, but by following larger, already successful brands, you will be able to get ahead by using their methods for your own benefit.

Advertising on Pinterest

Pinterest, like all other social media sites, offers the ability to create paid advertising by Promoting Pins. They also function quite similarly to Facebook or Twitter advertising, allowing for you to select from specific objectives in order to boost awareness, drive traffic or gain conversions. The question you may be asking, however, is whether or not it is worth it to pay for Pinterest advertising.

The main value that Pinterest provides is that the users are highly intentional. As Pinterest itself mentions "Unlike other platforms, Pinterest isn't about killing time. It's about finding something to do or buy." This means that you will, by default, be dealing with a population of users who are less resistant to conversion than other platforms. Facebook and Twitter both require a steady amount of convincing to get users to move, as they aren't on those sites for the purpose of making purchases. In fact, if you outright attempt to advertise to those types, you may even face resentment. The fact that Pinterest alone has a stronger conversion rate means that your advertising dollar will go a bit farther in terms of both engagement and making sales.

Since people are looking to Pinterest to drive their consumption decisions, you will have more opportunities to make hard sales through Pinterest advertising. And on top of that, the pricing is fairly competitive with Facebook. You only pay per click or per impression, depending on the campaign goals that you've established. So really, if you have invested time and money into making good quality images for ad campaigns and you like using Pinterest, it's worth using their paid advertising.

Pinterest is a different beast from Instagram. While Instagram can be very self-focused, Pinterest is really about hobbies, crafts and creativity. People aren't logging into Pinterest to see what other people are up to, they are looking to see what people are creating. If you are selling products or ideas that aid in creation or are creations themselves, then Pinterest is the perfect social media outlet for you.

Chapter 12: Tips and Tricks to Succeed in Social Media Marketing

Regardless of the main platforms that you decide to use, whether it be Instagram, Facebook or Pinterest, there are universal principles that should be adhered to when it comes to finding success in social media marketing. Below are a list of tips and tricks that should be remembered in order to increase your chances of reaching real success through online marketing.

1: You cannot force viral

Just about every marketer has a dream of their content going viral. Some post, some picture or joke suddenly takes off and before you have a chance to react, a wave of attention comes flooding over your product and you've gained thousands of followers! Maybe your content makes it to the news somehow! That dream is shared by just about every content creator, but sometimes marketers get a little too dialed into that dream and begin to seriously pursue going viral.

You cannot force something to become viral. There is nothing wrong with hoping that your content takes off, but you simply never know what the outcome will be. Instead of wasting time and money on people who can promise that something will go viral, just focus on creating the best content that you can. Quality content speaks for itself. It is impossible to know ahead of time what will go viral and what won't.

2: Learn how memes work

A meme is a picture, often of a person or a dog, with captions on it, outlining an idea, often making jokes about some part of culture. Memes are one form of communication between individuals and when one becomes popular, it can circulate around on the internet quite quickly.

Some marketers see memes and think about creating their own, but misinterpret the purpose of the meme and create a meme that doesn't actually function. It is either unfunny or misunderstands how the meme itself is used. This lends to the picture that the marketer is either woefully out of touch, or worse, attempting to pander to a younger audience while missing the point.

You are not required to create or circulate memes, but a lot of social media relies on using these images as ways to communicate with each other. Memes are a great form of short, visual entertainment that usually conveys an idea quickly and effectively.

If you are so inclined to create your own, make sure that you understand the point of a popular meme. You can research memes easily enough by looking up their origins and use on websites like KnowYourMeme. These sites explain the point of a specific meme and teach the format of how they are used correctly.

This is an important step if you want to be dialed into the current internet culture. Meme misuse is often ridiculed by the younger generation, so if you are marketing to them, make sure that you are current on how their memes are functioning.

3: Don't blur the lines between paid and organic advertising

At the end of the day, if you want to sell your product, you are going to have to spend money on advertising. There really is no other way around it. As the adage goes, you have to spend money to make money. Some advertisers, however, look at social media as a way to circumvent paying for ad space. This belief changes the way advertisers interact with their followers. Instead of wanting to provide value, the scales quickly become tipped and the advertiser uses social media to market products.

Of course, algorithms punish this kind of behavior by lowering reach and preventing the marketer from being anywhere close to effective. And followers will quickly grow tired of the self-serving behavior and either unfollow or just stop paying attention to the advertiser's feeble attempts to make a sale.

If you want to have strong, effective marketing results, you will need to pay for advertising. The social media component will organically advertise for your product over time and you may gain sales simply by having a presence, but your actions on that platform are meant to reinforce the pain advertising. The two work together in tandem. The social media presence allows for you to connect, find a target market and answer questions and concerns. The paid marketing allows for you to directly put your ads in front of them, hopefully converting them.

4: Authenticity is Key

No matter what you are doing in your marketing, the key is to focus on being as honest and authentic as you can. If you genuinely don't care for memes, don't use them. If you loathe using Twitter each day, don't waste your energy on it. You don't have to do it all when marketing online, because if you are coming from an inauthentic place, people will be able to sniff it out. Instead of going against your passions, pursuing trends solely for the sake of making a buck, stay true to your heart and to your mission.

Social media isn't about convincing people to buy into your product, in reality, it is about convincing people to buy into you and what you are doing. If you are changing your image, just so people will be interested in your product, then they are buying into a fraud. There won't be much of an honest connection between you and your followers. Share your passions and look for the people who share them as well. This will create stronger relationships and will convert

5: Remember the 80/20 rule of social media

In order to prevent yourself from accidentally blurring the lines between organic and paid marketing, it is helpful to adhere to the 80/20 rule. Simply put, 80% of the posts that you make should be about providing value to other people. This means that the majority of your posts that you make on social media should be content the uplifts, elevates and assist's others. And 20% of your posts should be about yourself, your business or your products. This allows for you to a nice balance between helping others and helping yourself. If that ratio is skewed too much, you could end up looking like a shill.

So for every 10 posts that you make, 8 should be content that is valuable for the followers and 2 should be content that is valuable for you. Of course, you will want to spread this out so that self-promoting posts are peppered in here and there, sandwiched between other posts of excellent value.

6: Create a content calendar

You are most likely a very busy individual. Running a business takes a lot of work and running social media requires a lot of thoughtfulness in order to work effectively. Rather than try to plan your social media content day to day, which can be undoubtedly exhausting, you should work to develop a content calendar.

A content calendar is where you plan ahead all of the types of content that you will be posting, what platforms and when. Most of the time, it will be helpful to plan out all of the content that you intend to post on a visual document. There are plenty of online content calendars that can help with this planning process. Planning ahead is very important because it allows for you to create themed weeks. If you know that you will have a product launch in six weeks, your calendar can be full of small teasers and hints that something great is coming in the future.

7: Use a platform aggregator

Using multiple platforms can be exceptionally tiresome if you are working on your own. Spending time going from Twitter, to Pinterest and to Facebook in order to make your daily posts is not only time consuming, but it also wastes a lot of energy. Fortunately, there are companies out that work as platform aggregators, letting you make posts to select social media outlets from one single website. Some of these aggregators offer free services, with paid features that can save you valuable time. Websites like Hootsuite or Buffer allow for you to not only make posts through one website, but also to plan posts ahead of time. That means you can take the content calendar that you've developed and then prepare them to be posted, often days or weeks in advance.

This can significantly cut down on the amount of time you spend on social media making posts. That frees you up to instead focus on replying, commenting and getting back to your regular work. You can still engage with others in each platform, but you won't be required to constantly hop from platform to platform to get stuff done.

8: Create Evergreen Content

Evergreen is a term meaning that the content itself does not get old. This allows for you to reuse that content later on, even a few years from now. Evergreen content is useful for multiple reasons, the first is that no matter when a person accesses that content, it will not be out of date. For example, if you were to write a piece about pest control, making no mention to the current year or any references that would only make sense to a person during the current time period, you could potentially reuse that piece every single year.

It is important that as you work to create content that remains evergreen, as a way of cutting cost in the future. The more evergreen content that you develop, the less you will have to spend each year, as you can simply just recirculate what you already have. Now, admittedly, not every single piece of content that you make will be evergreen, as promotions end, tastes change and cultures shift, but you should at least strive to make as much evergreen as you can during the first few years of content creation.

9: Keep up with the news

Social media is a rapidly changing platform. Things can happen in the blink of an eye that radically changes the way advertisers look at certain platforms. A bad update, a poor decision by the CEO or a sudden lawsuit can drastically alter the outlooks of a social media outlet. There really is no way to prepare for the future of social media, but if you stay current on the news, you should be able to react appropriately. Policies can change and sometimes those policies can destroy a company that isn't paying attention to the news. You must be, in the social media world, like a shark, always moving in order to survive. So make sure that you are always checking in with the news, reading reports and paying attention to the shifts of the consumer mindset. People can quickly flock from one platform to another and if you aren't on top of your game, they might end up leaving you behind.

10: Don't stop posting

Regardless of what platform you have chosen, you must remember to keep posting as much as recommended. There are so many things out there that are constantly vying for a person's attention and long gaps can kill a person's interest in your brand. The posts don't always have to be top notch, high quality posts, they can be as simple as reposts, inspirational quotes or funny pictures, but what is important is that you don't have any sizable gaps in your posting schedule. You could be potentially losing out on reach, new likes or even website clicks!

11: Point towards the product

As a social media marketer, it can be exciting to see higher numbers of followers and page likes. Seeing a tweet suddenly take off and get thousands of likes can really make you happy and in turn, may aim you towards potentially focusing more and more on getting those sweet, sweet likes. However, likes, followers or retweets have no cash value. At the end of the day, you must stay on point. Your goal is to move people from your Facebook, Twitter or Instagram to the place where you are selling your goods or services. Likes and followers are simply a means of getting to what really matters.

Therefore, it is of the utmost importance to not waste time trying to move people from one social media platform to another. You may have a large Twitter following, but a small number of Facebook page likes. Instead of spending your time, effort and energy trying to get your Twitter followers to like you on Facebook, focus on getting them more interest in what you have to offer. There's nothing wrong with mentioning other platforms, but when you begin actively campaigning to move people from one platform to another, things start to get a little complicated. Ask yourself, would you rather a follower check out your website or follow you on another platform? Which one has the better chance of getting you a sale?

12: Have good web design

In general, your website is ultimately where you will want your audience to end up. The website will be where you sell your goods or services and as such, needs to look great. You don't have to spend a fortune on web design either, as there are plenty of websites that offer sleek templates or drag and drop design to save you money in the long run.

People aren't looking for much either, when it comes to web design. Clear navigation, a minimal amount of pop-ups and the ability to see what is most important quickly are all what customers want. Offensive color schemes, clutter and hard to navigate menus can all turn a customer against you. Some might even simply exit the website, rather than work to figure out how to get around. This might seem harsh, but you have to remember that you are competing against every other well designed website out there. People don't want to waste their time on a bad website when there are thousands of other, more functional ones to use.

One more note about web design: above all else, you need to make sure that your website loads quickly. Regardless of whether the traffic is coming from paid ads or from links clicked from your social media posts, people cannot abide by slow loading websites. In fact, it is estimated that nearly 40% leave a website if it takes more than three seconds to load. This abandonment rate is simply brutal. Make sure that you have a fast loading website, or you may end up losing 40% of traffic that you paid for!

13: Guest Blog

One great way to get your name, social media identity and brand out there is to get involved with guest blogging. Guest blogging involves either inviting someone who is well established to write a blog post on your website, or asking a well-established blog if you can write a post for them. The benefits of guest blogging are tremendous and can be mutually beneficial for both parties.

When a blogger writes on your blog, he will be transferring a portion of his audience to your website, which will make them aware of your brand and may lead to them reading more of your content. Likewise, if you get to write on his blog, there will now be a link leading back to your website that readers can then access. What makes this mutually beneficial is that you are both sharing your audiences with each other.

Of course, there is no guarantee that you will be able to find a guest blogger who will be interested. But at the same time, there is really no risk in trying to locate a blogger and then sending them an email, humbly making a request.

14: Images are valuable

They say that a picture is worth a thousand words, and in the case of social media, pictures can be worth much more than that. Large walls of text are often glazed over by readers, but an interesting or funny picture with some captions will quickly catch their eye. If you want to get more engagement and circulate your content around more, but you are finding your current results lacking, try to post more images.

15: Use virtual assistants

If you find that you are having trouble juggling your regular workload and social media, but don't want to hire a full-time social media coordinator, don't worry! You can always hire a virtual assistant to do the bulk of the busywork for you. By using a freelancing site, you can hire someone to work part-time or even on a task by task basis in order to lighten your workload. Most virtual assistants are familiar with social media and won't require much training. You can then go about instructing them with what content you want to be created or what type of posts you would like them to plan ahead. By outsourcing some of the busy work, you are then freed up to focus on other, more demanding tasks.

Conclusion

Social media marketing has opened the floodgates for thousands of small businesses, artists and independent operators to share their products with the world. With patience and discipline, it is possible to use the power of the collective to increase the market share and popularity of what you create. But like all things, marketing is a journey and there are perils and pitfalls. You may not end up seeing results right away, but don't be discouraged! Learning how to market through social media is easy, but mastering it takes a lot of time and effort. The more that you learn each day, through missteps and mistakes will teach you how to improve yourself.

There may be a temptation to look to your competitors and think "I'll never be as successful as them," but don't give in to those thoughts. This journey is not about other people or products, but about you and your unique vision. Social media, above all else, allow us to connect like-minded people together. Someone, somewhere out there is looking for exactly what you have. All you need to do is be willing to keep trying to find them. As long as you stay focused, study the data and keep posting, you can't fail! All it takes is time and discipline to build your business to be exactly what you envision it to be! Good luck!

Before we begin I have a free gift for you from Russell Brunson - for those of you that don't know Russell Brunson is, he's the man that created Click Funnels. In my opinion it's the best funnel website out there and it has also helped create the most millionaires. Any form of passive income you are going to build, you will 100% need to leverage funnels of some sort. If you're reading this book, then you want to be the best in your industry. This book will give you the play by play to have people PAYING you for your advice. I am able to give you his best selling book for free right down here. I only have a few copies left so please get them while you can. Just click this http://bit.ly/giftfunnelbook

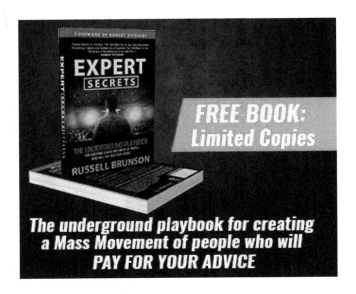